Eco-Conscious Living

Eco-Conscious Living

MAKING CHOICES THAT BENEFIT THE EARTH

Tristan Evergreen

QuantumQuill Press

Contents

Introduction

In a period set apart by developing natural difficulties, the idea of eco-cognizant living has changed from a specialty interest to a squeezing need. At its center, eco-cognizant living exemplifies the decisions and moves we initiate to limit our ecological impression, taking a stab at a concordance between our ways of life and the normal world. This way to deal with life allures us to think about not simply the prompt accommodation or cost of our decisions, however their effect in the world's wellbeing and the prosperity of people in the future.

The meaning of taking on an eco-cognizant way of life couldn't possibly be more significant. Each part of our day to day routines, from the food we devour to the methods of transportation we depend on, adds to a bigger picture that influences worldwide environments, environmental change, and biodiversity. The aggregate effect of individual activities has the ability to influence the equilibrium towards supportability or natural corruption. Hence, understanding and moderating our own and common ecological effects becomes an issue of moral decision as well as of endurance.

This book, is created to direct you through the excursion of understanding and carrying out reasonable practices in different aspects of life. It plans to enlighten the ways through which people can add to a bigger, positive natural change. By coordinating standards of maintainability into our schedules, we improve our personal satisfaction as well as take part in a worldwide development towards a more practical and impartial planet.

Organized to take special care of the two amateurs and those all around on the way of eco-cognizant living, this book unfurls through definite parts that cover crucial subjects like figuring out our natural effect, embracing practical living rudiments, and investigating roads for going past the essentials to impact significant change. Each segment is intended to give significant bits of knowledge and useful hints, making manageability a feasible objective for all.

As we dive into conversations on lessening waste, monitoring energy, reasonable eating, and eco-accommodating transportation, the book establishes the groundwork for essential manageable living practices. Pushing ahead, it ventures into further developed subjects like maintainable style, green financial planning, water preservation, and supporting biodiversity. Besides, it underlines the significance of local area commitment, backing, strategy change, and schooling in cultivating a supportable local area. At long last, sharing individual excursions and stories represents the genuine use of eco-cognizant living, offering motivation and inspiration to set out on or proceed with this satisfying excursion.

Setting out on an excursion towards eco-cognizant living is both an individual responsibility and an aggregate activity towards a more practical future. This book fills in as your aide, empowering you to ponder your day to day decisions, grasp their more extensive ramifications, and embrace the practices that contribute decidedly to the world's prosperity. As we investigate these subjects and techniques, recall that each little step counts. Together, our decisions and activities can produce a way towards a better planet and a more supportable conjunction with the regular world.

1

Chapter 1:
Understanding Our
Impact

The Carbon Impression Thought

The maxim "carbon impression" has transformed into an establishment in discussions about ecological change and legitimacy. It implies the total amount of ozone hurting substances, chiefly carbon dioxide, that are sent clearly or indirectly by individuals, affiliations, things, or events. These spreads add to an overall temperature modification and natural change, making the understanding and lessening of our carbon impression pressing for biological sensibility.

Each move we make, from driving a vehicle to warming our homes, incorporates the use of energy, a lot of which really comes from oil based goods. These activities release carbon dioxide and other ozone hurting substances into the climate, getting force and provoking the warming of our planet. The outcomes are far reaching, affecting weather patterns, sea levels, and organic frameworks all over the planet.

Processing one's carbon impression can be an edifying experience, uncovering what lifestyle choices clearly mean for the environment. A couple of web based smaller than usual PCs and instruments are open to help individuals and associations with surveying their petroleum derivative results, engaging more instructed decisions about energy use, transportation, and usage penchants.

Freeing the effects from natural change requires total movement to decrease our carbon impressions. This can incorporate direct changes, such as changing to energy-successful machines, reducing meat use, or settling on open transportation over confidential vehicles. For a greater degree, supporting harmless to the ecosystem power sources and maintaining for techniques that decrease petroleum product side-effects are essential steps toward a plausible future.

By getting it and expecting a feeling of pride with our carbon impression, we can seek after choices that benefit our own lives as well as add to an overall work to fight ecological change. The outing towards viability starts with care, and seeing our carbon impression is the main stage in making a huge difference.

Plastic Pollution and Its Repercussions

Plastic tainting has emerged as one of the most pressing environmental issues inside ongoing memory. With an enormous number of heaps of plastic waste entering our oceans consistently, the impact on marine life, natural frameworks, and human prosperity is critical. Plastic, as a result of its strong nature, can persist in the environment for a long time, provoking an example of defilement that is trying to break.

The convenience of plastic has provoked its widespread presence in our standard schedules, yet its evacuation presents immense troubles. Single-use plastics, similar to packs, containers, and straws, are the fundamental liable gatherings, every now and again ending up in streams and oceans, where they separate into microplastics. These little particles are ingested by marine animals, entering the dominance hierarchy and potentially impacting human prosperity.

Combatting plastic pollution requires a mind boggling technique. Diminishing use of single-use plastics, further creating waste organization structures, and supporting the improvement of biodegradable choices are key frameworks. Individuals can have an impact by embracing reusable things, partaking in area clean up tries, and pushing for methodologies that limit plastic creation and enable reusing.

The fight against plastic pollution isn't just about shielding marine life and saving ordinary eminence; it's connected to ensuring a superior planet for individuals later on. By understanding the results of our plastic use and taking action to direct its impact, we can help with stemming the tide of pollution and move towards a more plausible world.

Biodiversity Hardship

Biodiversity, the grouping of life in the world, is key for the prosperity and relentlessness of natural frameworks. It maintains everything from food security and clean water to irresistible anticipation and climate rule. Regardless, human activities, similar to deforestation, defilement, and natural change, are causing an outstanding loss of biodiversity, compromising the perseverance of incalculable species and the organic frameworks that depend upon them.

The explanations behind biodiversity setback are perplexing, but they are generally determined by the expansion of cultivating, metropolitan development, and the misleading of customary resources. These activities crush regular environmental elements as well as area conditions, making it difficult for species to scrape by and mimic. Ecological change deteriorates these strains, changing regular environmental factors and disturbing the delicate harmony of natural frameworks.

The results of biodiversity setback are broad, impacting the species in peril as well as human peoples. Organic frameworks crippled by the lack of biodiversity are less prepared to offer the sorts of help whereupon we depend, similar to treatment, water cleaning, and carbon sequestration. Furthermore, biodiversity is a wellspring of genetic materials indispensable for medicine, cultivating, and industry.

Addressing biodiversity setback requires an organized work to shield and restore conditions, complete viable land-use practices, and ease natural change. This can be achieved through the underpinning of defended districts, the progression of biodiversity-obliging developing, and the assistance of insurance drives. Individuals can contribute by supporting conservation affiliations, making affordable customer choices, and exposing issues about the meaning of biodiversity.

Understanding our impact on the planet is the most fundamental push toward embracing a more eco-discerning lifestyle. By becoming aware of the repercussions of our carbon impression, the results of plastic pollution, and the meaning of saving biodiversity, we can begin to make choices that benefit ourselves as well as the Earth. As we push ahead, let us embrace the commitment of dealing with our planet with care, ensuring a possible and prospering world from here onward, indefinitely.

2

Chapter 2:
Sustainable Living
Basics

Diminishing Waste

In the mission for practicality, lessening waste stands separated as an essential and reachable goal. The mantra "Diminish, Reuse, Reuse" offers a direct yet convincing design for restricting our biological impression. By focusing in first on diminishing what we consume, we clearly decline how much waste made and the resources expected for creation and expulsion.

Diminishing waste requires a discerning work to investigate our necessities versus needs. It incorporates choosing things with insignificant packaging, picking better standards regardless of anything else, and avoiding single-use things for reusable different choices. Clear changes, for example, conveying a reusable water bottle, shopping with material sacks, and using refillable compartments, can basically kill plastic waste.

Past confidential usage, reducing waste also suggests monitoring food waste. Orchestrating suppers, buying exactly what we need, and sorting out some way to save or creatively use additional items are practices that add to a waste-diminishing lifestyle. Treating the dirt normal waste further abatements the load on landfills, returning critical enhancements to the soil.

Reducing waste isn't just an exhibit of normal insurance; it's a declaration of standard against the disposable culture that adds to overall tainting. By taking on a more cautious method for managing usage, we can show others how its finished, moving others to contemplate the impact of their choices and developing a culture of reasonability.

Energy Capability at Home

Energy capability is a groundwork of reasonable living, offering both biological and financial benefits. By propelling how we use energy in our homes, we can through and through diminish ozone hurting substance outpourings and get a good deal on help bills. The outing toward energy capability begins with direct advances that can have a tremendous impact after some time.

One of the most straightforward approaches to additional creating energy efficiency is by changing to Drove lighting. LEDs consume an irrelevant piece of the energy of traditional brilliant bulbs and last fundamentally longer, diminishing both energy use and waste. Redesigning home security is another strong measure, as it restricts the lack of power in winter and keeps homes cooler in summer, in like manner reducing the necessity for warming and cooling.

Energy-capable machines similarly expect a basic part. Right when this present time is the best opportunity to supersede or upgrade devices, picking models with high energy capability assessments can provoke colossal venture assets and lower petroleum derivative side-effects. Likewise, embracing penchants, for instance, changing out lights while not being utilized, switching off electronic devices that are not being charged, and using adroit indoor controllers can propel energy utilize all through the home.

Placing assets into harmless to the ecosystem power sources, similar to daylight based chargers, can moreover grow a home's energy efficiency and legitimacy. Though the fundamental endeavor may be higher, the excessively long speculation assets and regular benefits make harmless to the ecosystem power a certainly engaging decision for eco-discerning home loan holders.

By zeroing in on energy viability, we not simply add to the fight against natural change yet furthermore embrace a lifestyle that values resource security and environmental stewardship. These exercises, when copied across networks, can provoke huge reductions in energy usage and ozone draining substance releases all over the planet.

Attainable Dietary examples

Attainable eating is connected to picking food sources that are a good idea for both the planet and our bodies. It incorporates pondering how food is made, took care of, and moved, and going with choices that limit biological impact. Indispensable to efficient eating is the diminishing of meat use, particularly red and dealt with meats, which have a colossal carbon and water impression in view of the resources expected for tamed creatures developing.

Taking on a plant-based diet, whether or not exclusively, can drastically reduce one's carbon impression. Plant-based food assortments generally require less water, land, and energy to convey than animal based food assortments. Coordinating more normal items, vegetables, vegetables, and grains into feasts helps the environment as well as supports a strong and contrasted diet.

Sensible eating in like manner suggests picking area and periodic produce at whatever point what is going on permits. This reduces the non-renewable energy source results related with huge distance food transport and supports close by farmers and economies. What's more, buying regular food sources can add to soil prosperity and biodiversity, as normal developing practices avoid the usage of designed pesticides and excrements.

Restricting food waste is another essential piece of legitimate eating. By organizing meals, taking care of food properly, and using additional items inventively, individuals can on a very basic level decrease how much food that goes to waste. This conservatives resources as well as diminishes methane releases from disintegrating food in landfills.

Embracing plausible dietary examples is areas of strength for a for influencing the food structure towards extra innocuous to the environment practices. Through cautious choices about what we eat, we can maintain a food system that upholds the two people and the planet.

Eco-obliging Transportation

Transportation is a huge ally of overall non-renewable energy source results, making eco-obliging travel choices crucial for diminishing our regular impact. Viable transportation choices like walking, cycling, and using public travel decline defilement as well as recommendation prosperity and neighborhood.

Walking and cycling are the most innocuous to the biological system strategies for transportation. They produce zero outpourings, decrease gridlock, and advance genuine prosperity. For those living in metropolitan areas, these decisions can every now and again be speedier and more accommodating for short distances than driving.

Public transportation is another sensible choice. Transports, trains, and streetcars basically decline the per-individual carbon impression of development by splitting the trip between various voyagers. By picking public travel over confidential vehicles, individuals can add to cut down non-renewable energy source results and diminished interest for oil based goods.

For longer distances or when various decisions are not reachable, vehicle sharing and picking electric or creamer vehicles can ease natural impact. Electric vehicles (EVs), constrained by harmless to the ecosystem power, offer a promising choice rather than traditional fuel energized vehicles, with the likelihood to reduce ozone draining substance releases from the transportation region tremendously.

Embracing eco-obliging transportation strategies isn't simply a phase towards legitimacy yet moreover an opportunity to reconsider our relationship with development. By zeroing in on decisions that benefit the environment, we can help with driving the advancement towards an extra sensible and related world.

3

Chapter 3: Going Beyond the Basics

Manageable Design

Manageable design difficulties the quick style industry's standards by pushing for moral assembling, material obtaining, and buyer conduct. The quick design model, described by fast creation cycles and minimal expense articles of clothing, contributes altogether to ecological debasement and work abuse. Conversely, manageable design centers around making garments that limit natural effect and guarantee fair working circumstances.

One critical part of practical style is the selection of materials. Supportable brands frequently utilize natural cotton, reused textures, and other eco-accommodating materials that require less water and synthetic compounds to create than ordinary materials. Also, these brands underline sturdiness and ageless plan, empowering shoppers to purchase less, greater things that last longer.

Buyers can take part in reasonable style by embracing a more careful way to deal with shopping. This incorporates purchasing less however picking great, supporting moral brands, and taking into account second-hand or classic dress as suitable and chic choices. Fixing and upcycling garments likewise assume a critical part in broadening the existence of pieces of clothing and diminishing waste.

The development towards reasonable design isn't just about changing how we purchase garments; it's tied in with changing our relationship with style. It provokes us to esteem higher standards no matter what, to think about the narratives behind our articles of clothing, and to settle on decisions that regard the two individuals and the planet.

Green Money management

Green money management addresses the convergence of money and ecological manageability. It includes distributing capital towards organizations, ventures, and innovations that add to a more supportable world. As consciousness of natural issues develops, more financial backers are looking for open doors that offer monetary returns as well as emphatically affect the planet.

Green ventures can take many structures, including environmentally friendly power projects, economical farming, clean innovation, and organizations with solid ecological, social, and administration (ESG) rehearses. By coordinating assets towards these areas, financial backers can uphold the change to a low-carbon economy, advance asset protection, and encourage development in supportability.

For individual financial backers inspired by green money management, there are a few choices to consider. Shared assets and trade exchanged reserves (ETFs) zeroed in on manageability subjects offer expanded openness to green speculations. Then again, direct interest in green bonds or loads of organizations driving in supportability rehearses considers more designated influence.

Green money management expects a reasonable level of effort

to guarantee that speculations line up with manageability objectives. This might include investigating organizations' supportability reports, figuring out their ESG appraisals, and remaining educated about the more extensive effects regarding their tasks. In spite of these difficulties, green financial planning offers the double advantage of adding to a more practical future while possibly producing solid returns.

Water Preservation Methods

Water is a valuable asset, yet its preservation is many times ignored in conversations of maintainability. Productive water use is pivotal for diminishing weight on freshwater sources, saving biological systems, and alleviating the impacts of dry seasons and water shortage. From basic propensities at home to local area wide drives, there are various ways of preserving water.

At the singular level, lessening water utilization can be accomplished through day to day practices like scrubbing down, fixing spills instantly, and utilizing water-proficient apparatuses. In the nursery, utilizing dry spell safe plants, rehearsing water gathering, and using trickle water system frameworks can altogether diminish water use.

Past private activities, supporting and executing practical water the board arrangements at the neighborhood and public levels are fundamental. This can incorporate pushing for the security of wetlands, which normally channel and store water, and supporting framework projects that advance proficient water use and reusing.

Water preservation isn't simply a question of asset the board; it's a basic part of worldwide natural supportability. By embracing water-saving practices and supporting strategies that safeguard water assets, people and networks can add to a more feasible and water-secure future.

Supporting Biodiversity

Biodiversity, the assortment of life on The planet, supports the wellbeing and usefulness of environments. Notwithstanding, human exercises have prompted a fast decrease in biodiversity, undermining environment administrations and human prosperity. Supporting biodiversity is in this way a vital part of going past the nuts and bolts of manageability.

People can uphold biodiversity in different ways, beginning with their own nurseries or local area green spaces. Establishing local species, making pollinator-accommodating natural surroundings, and keeping away from the utilization of hurtful pesticides can transform even little spaces into biodiversity areas of interest. Also, partaking in or supporting nearby protection projects, for example, wetland reclamation or tree establishing drives, can emphatically affect neighborhood and local biodiversity.

On a more extensive scale, pushing for strategies that safeguard normal living spaces, imperiled species, and advance manageable land use is indispensable. This can include supporting preservation associations, taking part in open conversations, and deciding in favor of pioneers focused on ecological security.

Supporting biodiversity isn't simply a natural goal; it's an interest in our aggregate future. By making moves to secure and upgrade biodiversity, we can assist with guaranteeing the versatility of environments whereupon all life depends.

4

Chapter 4: Building a Sustainable Community

Drawing in with Your People group

Making a practical local area includes more than individual activities; it requires aggregate exertion and commitment. It begins with igniting discussions about supportability inside your own circles — family, companions, and neighbors. These conversations can bring issues to light, share information, and rouse aggregate activity towards more eco-cognizant practices.

Local area commitment can take many structures, from coordinating nearby tidy up endeavors to partaking in manageability studios and occasions. Such exercises add to natural improvement as well as cultivate a feeling of local area and common perspective. In addition, by including neighborhood organizations and schools in these drives, the scope and effect of these endeavors can be fundamentally enhanced.

Building a practical local area likewise implies supporting neighborhood economies. Shopping at neighborhood ranchers' business sectors, visiting private ventures, and partaking in local area upheld agribusiness (CSA) projects can decrease carbon impressions and support nearby economies. These activities energize the creation and utilization of nearby, maintainable products, making a versatile and interconnected local area.

Additionally, captivating with neighborhood government and policymakers is urgent. Upholding for practical metropolitan preparation, environmentally friendly power reception, and green spaces can prompt foundational changes that help a maintainable local area. Through petitions, going to board gatherings, or in any event, campaigning for nearby position, people can impact strategy and add to establishing a more practical climate for all.

Backing and Strategy Change

Support assumes a urgent part in driving ecological strategy change. By raising our voices for supportability, we can impact the choices that shape our networks and the more extensive world. Powerful promotion includes teaching ourselves on ecological issues, speaking with policymakers, and activating others to make a move.

One viable road for backing is through partaking in or sorting out crusades that emphasis on unambiguous ecological issues, like environmentally friendly power reception, squander decrease, or preservation endeavors. These missions can incorporate composing letters or messages to chose authorities, taking part in tranquil shows, or utilizing online entertainment stages to bring issues to light and compel policymakers to act.

Building alliances and associations with other ecological gatherings, local area associations, and organizations can intensify support endeavors. These coordinated efforts can make a unified front, settling on the decision for change harder to overlook. Besides, captivating with the media to feature significant issues and activities can contact a more extensive crowd, pressing policymakers to act.

Remaining informed and deciding in favor of pioneers who focus on ecological maintainability is one more significant part of promotion. Choosing agents who are focused on tending to environmental change, safeguarding regular assets, and carrying out green approaches can prompt huge advancement in building manageable networks.

Training and Effort

Training is the establishment whereupon feasible networks are constructed. Educating people about the significance regarding manageability and how to integrate eco-cognizant practices into their lives can groundbreakingly affect a local area. Outreach projects, studios, and workshops can give the information and abilities expected to make feasible living available to everybody.

Schools can incorporate manageability into their educational programs, showing understudies ecological issues and arrangements since the beginning. Public venues and libraries can have speakers and show materials connected with supportability, offering assets for learned. Online stages and virtual entertainment likewise offer tremendous open doors for spreading information and drawing in with a more extensive crowd.

Chipping in for neighborhood natural associations or drives can give active experience and further training. These encounters add to self-awareness as well as reinforce local area ties and advance a culture of supportability.

In addition, teaching the local area about the financial, natural, and medical advantages of feasible living can spur activity. At the point when individuals comprehend the substantial advantages of maintainability, for example, diminished energy costs, better ways of life, and a cleaner climate, they are bound to embrace and promoter for supportable practices.

Feasible Strategic approaches

Organizations assume a pivotal part in building economical networks. By taking on supportable practices, organizations can lessen their natural effect, work on their notorieties, and contribute decidedly to their networks. This incorporates carrying out energy-productive activities, diminishing waste, obtaining feasible materials, and supporting fair work rehearses.

Empowering work environments to become environmentally viable can begin with basic advances, for example, decreasing paper use, reusing, and saving energy. Organizations can likewise focus on additional tremendous changes, such as taking on environmentally friendly power sources, putting resources into manageable foundation, and guaranteeing their inventory chains focus on ecological and social obligation.

Supporting or beginning eco-accommodating organizations is one more method for adding to a practical local area. These organizations give reasonable items and administrations as well as act as models for mindful practices. They show the way that benefit and supportability can remain closely connected, empowering different organizations to stick to this same pattern.

Customers play a strong part in this cycle by supporting organizations that are focused on supportability. By deciding to burn through cash on items and administrations that line up with eco-cognizant qualities, customers can drive interest for supportable practices and urge more organizations to embrace green drives.

Chapter 5: Personal Journey to Eco-Conscious Living

Setting out on a way toward eco-cognizant living is both a profoundly private and generally effective excursion. It includes a change in context, propensities, and frequently, values. This part digs into my own excursion towards manageability, featuring the difficulties confronted, arrangements found, and the continuous course of learning and adjusting for a more practical way of life.

The Enlivening

My process started with an enlivening, an acknowledgment of the obvious truth of our natural emergency. It was a slow cycle, powered by narratives, articles, and firsthand perceptions of waste, contamination, and ecological debasement. This mindfulness brought a feeling of obligation; I could as of now not live in obliviousness of the effect of my decisions in the world. The craving to have an effect, regardless of how little, turned into the main thrust behind my excursion toward eco-cognizant living.

Making Changes

The initial steps included unmistakable changes to diminish my natural impression. I began with straightforward activities: conveying reusable packs, jugs, and holders; diminishing meat utilization; and preserving energy and water at home. Each step, however little, felt like a triumph. Notwithstanding, challenges were inescapable. Conquering the comfort of dispensable items, tracking down reasonable manageable other options, and changing in accordance with a plant-based diet required exertion, research, and in some cases, split the difference.

Going Further

As my process advanced, my activities went past essential changes. I investigated economical design, choosing second-hand and morally made dress, and dug into green financial planning, supporting organizations and tasks with a positive ecological effect. I additionally took part in nearby preservation endeavors, understanding the significance of local area in accomplishing more extensive natural objectives. These more profound changes were not just about limiting damage; they were about effectively adding to positive change.

The Continuous Excursion

Eco-cognizant living is a continuous excursion, not an objective. It's about constant picking up, adjusting, and tracking down better approaches to live as one with the planet. Challenges stay, for example, exploring social circumstances, offsetting accommodation with manageability, and remaining propelled despite worldwide ecological issues. In any case, the prizes — further developed well-being, a feeling of direction, and the information that I'm adding to a more prominent great — far offset the hardships.

Considering my excursion, I've understood that eco-cognizant living isn't about flawlessness however progress. It's tied in with pursuing better decisions, slowly but surely, and motivating others to do likewise. This excursion has shown me the force of individual activities joined with aggregate endeavors. Together, we can make a more practical world, as far as ourselves might be concerned, however for people in the future.

Conclusion

As we finish up "Eco-Cognizant Living: Settling on Decisions that Advantage the Earth," we consider the excursion embraced — a journey through the domains of supportability, grounded in the force of individual and aggregate activity. This book has woven through the essentials of living reasonably, wandered into the domains of cutting edge rehearses, and highlighted the crucial job of local area commitment and individual responsibility. It has pointed to illuminate as well as to motivate; to not just aide however to stir activity towards a more manageable presence.

Leaving on a way toward eco-cognizant living is both an individual decision and an aggregate goal. We've investigated the heap ways our day to day routines cross with the climate — from the food we eat and the garments we wear to the ventures we make and the networks we help construct. Every section has enlightened the potential for influence inborn in these crossing points, offering viable moves toward proceed all the more delicately on the Earth while enhancing our own lives and those of people in the future.

However, the excursion doesn't end here. Manageability is an advancing exchange between our developing information in the world's necessities and our ability for advancement and sympathy. It is a way produced by continuous learning, variation, and the eagerness to take part in the complex, once in a while testing, cycles of progress. The story of eco-cognizant living is consistently composed, with each activity, every decision, adding to a bigger story of trust and flexibility.

This book has additionally highlighted the meaning of local

area in the supportability condition. Maintainable living, in its substance, is a mutual undertaking — an embroidery of individual activities woven into an aggregate power for natural stewardship. By drawing in with our networks, upholding for maintainable strategies, teaching others, and supporting green organizations, we enhance the effect of our decisions, producing a common vision for an economical future.

In the impression of our process lies the comprehension that supportability isn't an objective yet a consistent course of development and improvement. It is tied in with doing all that can be expected with what we have, realizing that each step made is a stride towards a better planet. The difficulties of living economically are matched by the significant open doors for advancement, association, and recharging. As we push ahead, let us convey the bits of knowledge and motivations from these pages into our lives, embracing the delights and obligations of eco-cognizant living.

"Eco-Cognizant Living: Going with Decisions that Advantage the Earth" is in excess of an aide; it's a greeting. An encouragement to see the world with new eyes, to perceive our ability to impact change, and to step strongly towards a future where people reside as one with the normal world. As we close this part, another opens — a section of activity, trust, and proceeded with obligation to the earth that supports us.

Together, we have the ability to shape a feasible world. Our decisions today will reverberate through ages, a demonstration of our regard for the planet and one another. Allow us to pick shrewdly, with hearts and psyches open to the vast potential outcomes of a practical tomorrow.

Additional Resources

Setting out on the way to eco-cognizant living is a compensating venture that benefits both the individual and the planet. To additional help your excursion, an abundance of assets is accessible that can extend your comprehension, motivate activity, and interface you with similar networks. The following are painstakingly chosen assets to direct you in different parts of maintainable living.

Books

1. "This Changes Everything: Capitalism vs. The Climate" by Naomi Klein - A convincing investigation of the connection between natural debasement and financial works on, offering bits of knowledge into revolutionary strategy changes and developments.
2. "The Zero Waste Lifestyle: Live Well by Throwing Away Less" by Amy Korst - Gives useful hints to decreasing family squander, stressing the significance of little changes with a major effect.
3. "Cradle to Cradle: Remaking the Way We Make Things" by William McDonough & Michael Braungart - A weighty book that reconsiders item plan standards for natural supportability.

Websites and Online Platforms

- The Environmental Working Group (EWG) - Offers

resources for reducing exposure to chemicals and living a healthier, more sustainable lifestyle. (www.ewg.org)
- TreeHugger - A leading media outlet dedicated to driving sustainability mainstream, covering a wide range of topics from green design to natural sciences. (www.treehugger.com)
- The Minimalists - Provides inspiration and tips for living a meaningful life with less, focusing on decluttering and mindful consumption. (www.theminimalists.com)

Apps and Tools

- Good On You - A mobile app that rates the ethical and environmental impact of clothing brands, helping you make informed fashion choices.
- Ecosia - A search engine that uses its profits to plant trees. By essentially looking through the web, you can add to reforestation endeavors.
- OLIO - Connects neighbors with each other and with local businesses so surplus food and other items can be shared, not thrown away.

Organizations to Support or Volunteer For

- The Nature Conservancy - Works around the globe to protect ecologically important lands and waters for nature and people. Volunteering or donating can support their conservation efforts.
- 350.org - An international movement working to end the use of fossil fuels and transition to renewable energy. They organize grassroots campaigns on a global scale.
- Local environmental groups and initiatives - Engaging with local environmental organizations can make a tangible

difference in your community. Consider volunteering for tree planting events, beach clean-ups, or community gardening projects.

Staying Informed and Engaged

As you proceed your eco-cognizant living excursion, remaining educated and drew in with the local area will be imperative. Go to studios, join neighborhood natural gatherings, and take part in web-based discussions to share encounters and gain from others. Keep in mind, the progress to a more manageable way of life is a slow cycle, loaded up with learning valuable open doors and snapshots of reflection. By using these assets, you're moving toward going with decisions that benefit both you and the Earth.

This rundown is only a beginning stage. The field of maintainability is immense and always advancing, so keep on searching out new data, challenge yourself to develop, and share your insight with others. Together, we can have a tremendous effect on the strength of our planet.